MW01702252

WISDOM:
THE HIDDEN TREASURE

Understanding Why God Not Only Sent His Son, But He Also Left His Book!

To: Dr. N. Marchi,

May the Unending Wisdom of God continue to be your portion...

Happy Reading!!

Always,

Rev. Henrietta C. Ekekezie

April 17, 2023

WISDOM: The Hidden Treasure
Understanding Why God Not Only Sent His Son, But He Also Left His Book!

Certain pronouns capitalized in Scripture that refer to the Father, Son and Holy Spirit is the author's choice as well as emphasis within Scripture quotations.

www.RefreshingGloryMinistries.org

ISBN: 978-0-692-84865-4

Library of Congress In Publication Data

Category: Self-Help / Motivational & Inspirational / Faith / Wisdom

---

Written by: Henrietta C. Ekekezie | info@refreshinggloryministries.org

Edited by: Miriam Mèndez & Jahshua E. Blyden

Cover Design: Jamel Kornegay

Formatted by: Eli Blyden | CrunchTime Graphics for Publishing

Printed in the United States of America by: A&A Printing & Publishing

Dedication

This book is dedicated to My Lord and Savior Jesus Christ, My Mighty Fortress and The Wind underneath my wings.

To the human heart that struggles to find the joy, fulfillment and satisfaction of God's wisdom.

To my late irreplaceable parents, Mr. Obed Maduegbunam and Madam Rhoda Chiegeteokwu Ekekezie, who instilled in me the discipline, inherent in the Word of God. Their further deposit on the power of love, wisdom, contentment and courage into my life cannot be measured. I am what and who I am today, because of these priceless investments. They remain my gems!

To my precious Refreshing Glory Ministries family, your passion to know more drove me to dig deeper into the table of truth. I want you to know your fellowship is a very cherished part of my life. I'm deeply grateful for the gift of each of you.

To Apostle Joshua and Pastor Ify Nathan, and the congregation at Glory Center Family Church, your inspiration, prophetic prayers, love and support. I value each of you and the fellowship we share. The altar of this house will always have a special place in my heart.

To Ambassador Marjorie R. Kornegay, for your inspiration, love, prayers and immense support. I want you to know that I recognize you and your family, as one of the best gifts I have, in the call of God. You are so nice to know and I deeply appreciate you.

To Reverend Dr. Gertie L. Hurley, for your insightful guidance, inspiration and love in bringing this vision to reality. I'm immensely grateful.

To Pastor Portia F. Tyler, for your love, prayers and encouragement all through this project. My love and thanks to you.

To Saba, Teddy, Naomi and Nathan, for your tireless support, sacrifice and dedication towards completion of this project. When I count my blessings, I count you as one.

To Ego, Augusta, who helped me, prayed and encouraged me along the way. I cherish your friendship, love and devotion over the years and I deeply thank you.

To Reverend Pauline Okoroji, my Spiritual Mother and the ICN family, Pastor Doreen, Codelia and many more, for speaking growth into my life.

To my special siblings, Late Mrs. Josephine Diribe, Chike Ekekezie and surviving siblings, Mrs. Patricia Izuchukwu and Professor (Dr.) Ike Ekekezie, your significance in my life cannot be put into words. You brought and continue to bring amazing joy and love to my world. My Destiny story will not be complete without you. I love you dearly!

To my brother in- law Mr. Ben Izuchukwu, for your encouragement through the years, and fuelling my vision with prayer and support. I'm deeply grateful.

To my nephews, nieces, grand and great nephews, grand and great nieces, cousins, God children and Spiritual children, I'd like to let you know it takes more than a desire, to fulfill God's purpose for your life. It sure does take some Spiritual strength. Allow the Spirit of

God as you read these chapters to illuminate the areas in your life, which need to be subdued with Godly wisdom. Then, decisively determine to make your life and ministry a spiritual success that will not only bring glory to God, but will also bless the nations of the earth. I urge you, therefore, to ensure you run a good race, to finish strong! You are my treasures!

To my many friends who support me daily in real life through personal contacts, phone calls, emails and other social media outlets. I applaud each of you.

Endorsement

The obvious branding of grace and wisdom of God in the life of Minister Henrietta (Sister Etta) Ekekezie, is both amazing and rare. Her further uncovering to the world, as well as I have known her all too well over the past two decades, as her pastor, will build up into an undeniable generational impact. She humbly and faithfully lives a devoted life, truly exudes what she has distilled in this book about “Revealing Wisdom as a Hidden Treasure".

Make no mistakes about it, Wisdom is the Principal Thing! Wisdom is a Spirit, the Principal Spirit of God. It is often personalized and perfectly fits the Personhood of Jesus Christ (1 Corinthians 1:30), who indwells every believer by His Spirit (Colossians 1:27) as the Hope of Glory! If, therefore, Wisdom is the Personhood of Christ, He can also be engaged through a Relationship of Intimacy, predicated on God's kind of faith. Such relationship originates in salvation experience and continues through daily encounter in Him. It's like a deep ocean that finds its small beginning from the rock's cleft, which springs into ankle deep streams. May this book navigate you into a new and deeper walk in the Wisdom of God that will usher in His Refreshing Glory, into your life. I know it will.

Shalom!

Apostle Joshua O. Nathan, Sr.
Senior Pastor | Glory Center Family Church
Lanham, MD 20774

Table of Contents

Foreword

I am honored that Minister Henrietta (Prophetess, Sister Etta) Ekekezie, a great "Woman of God" asked me to write this foreword. She uses her gift of prophecy to edify the Body of Christ. I had the privilege of meeting Minister Etta over 15 years ago, and am delighted to refer to her as my "little sister." I have witnessed over several years her birthing, nurturing, and developing the Ministry of Refreshing Glory, which incidentally has several components; Spiritual Kitchen, and mentoring of women in their various and diverse walks of life.

She serves as an Empowerment Coach, mentor, leader, and teacher to many women who seek her for prayer, leadership, guidance, encouragement and wisdom. Her most recent endeavor is this God ordained book entitled "Wisdom - the Hidden Treasure" which will bless you. This book is filled with biblical wisdom from God's Word, the Holy Bible. Minister Etta gives you a thorough and in-depth understanding of "Wisdom" and its value to the Believer.

You will readily note that this book is scripturally based, and written to enlighten everyone about wisdom.

We, her family and friends are so excited because this book is only the first of many books to follow, and authored by Minister Etta.

~ Ambassador Marjorie R. Kornegay
John 3:16 Christian Bookstore, CEO

My Inspiration

I wrote the book because I came to realize that no one can know the things God has put in your heart if it's not written down. No one is a mind reader. It's good to document ones thoughts. Your book is your aroma. Your book is your fragrance. It is your presence. Your book is your experience. Your book is you. Your book will bless many. Everybody will not read your book, not because they dislike you, but because you are not called to affect their lives. Whichever way it goes, it still must be written. Your book is your legacy. Your book outlives you. Your book will go where you may never go. Your book will help millions who when they read it, will receive invaluable insight that will help them overcome whatever challenges they may be going through. Your book is a GPS (Global Positioning System) to many.

The insights shared in this book will enable many to set boundary lines on their past, and move forward confidently with God, to a strong finish. God gave us eyes, and He made sure it's strategically placed in front of our faces. Have you ever wondered why? I feel it's because He wants us to forget those things which are behind, and press forward to our future. How sad it will be, to have eyes, and not see. Helen Keller, a blind woman said, “The only thing worse than being blind is having sight but no vision.” Even in her blindness, she could see! This is the power of inner vision! Looking and seeing beyond the mundane, and adversity! May you not be one of those who look, but cannot see. You don’t drive forward with your gear in reverse, neither do you drive forward looking in your rear view mirror. I urge you, that even in apparent failure, fail forward. When you finally get up, you will only be looking ahead, and reaching further to get back on your feet, not backwards.

WISDOM:
THE HIDDEN TREASURE

Understanding Why God Not Only Sent His Son,
But He Also Left His Book!

INTRODUCTION

Revealing Wisdom As A Hidden Treasure

Have you ever wondered why God not only sent His Son, but He also left His book - the Bible for us to read? Have you ever wondered why He said in Proverbs 4:7 that, "Wisdom is the principal thing; therefore, get wisdom: and with all thy getting, get understanding." Have you ever wondered why in James 1:5 He said, "If any of you lack wisdom, let him ask of God that giveth to all men liberally, and upbraideth not; and it shall be given him." Have you ever bothered to know why He said in Proverbs 1:7 that, "The fear of the Lord is the beginning of wisdom?" Many will be wondering what wisdom is, and why all this talk about wisdom? My question to us is, why not wisdom? If the Word of God tells us wisdom is the principal thing, it is irrevocably the principal thing. It is law to all who believe. Even the Webster's Dictionary describes "principal" as the "first in rank or importance. God is a researcher. He knew way back that we will need help with finding out all there is to know about everything in life; of which wisdom is paramount hence, He left His Book. Joshua 1:8 says, "This book of the law shall not depart out of your mouth, but you shall meditate on it day and night, that you may observe to do according to all that is written in it. For then you shall make your way prosperous, and then you shall deal wisely and have good success." The bible truly is irreplaceable. It is the greatest resource manual for every facet of life. It would have been an absolute chaos, had He not left His book for us. Thank God He did!

CHAPTER ONE

What Is Wisdom?

Webster's Dictionary describes wisdom as, "good judgment." I personally feel it is the God empowering ability, to have an in-depth understanding of issues, however intricate, through insight and ultimately make sensible decisions. Job 28:28 says, "The fear of the Lord, that is Wisdom." In Proverbs 3:18, Wisdom is described as a tree of life. Every tree has a root, a stem, and a crown. If wisdom is likened to a tree, that means it has a root, a stem, and a branch. The root is the part of the tree that remains underground, it's primary function is to hold the tree, absorb water, and minerals from the soil. The stem is the trunk of a tree, it separates the roots from the leaves. It also transports nutrients from the soil to the leaves. The crown consists of the leaves and the branches at the top. The leaves are responsible for photosynthesis. The branches are the side shoots originating from the buds. Developed buds produce shoots with leaves, whose growth will lead to a full branch.

If wisdom is described as a tree of life, and I know God is too wise to make mistakes, that means, it also has a root, a stem, and a crown like every other tree.

The root of the tree is the anchor. Wisdom, as a tree of life, with an obvious root, means our lives must be anchored in the wisdom of God, received through meditating constantly on His Word. This not only nourishes our minds, but also gives us guidance and stability in our undertakings in life.

The stem of the wisdom tree transports God-nutrients, or nuggets such as humility, love, wisdom and peace drawn from the root and soil of the Word; to help us grow wisely different aspects of our lives. These nuggets are our Path-Finder and much more. When we imbibe them in our daily lives, they help us make good decisions, which consequently will lead to our enjoying healthy relationships, ministries, and careers to mention just a few. We ultimately visibly blossom, and become a blessing to our generation.

The crown portion of the wisdom tree is where we begin to bud, and develop branches. Here, due to maturity, we begin to branch out into other nations and continents. Through the grace and wisdom of God, various ministries are thus established, to support, bring hope to the hopeless, thereby becoming a refuge, and shelter from the storm for many. Even Proverbs 1:7 also says that, "the fear of the Lord is the beginning of wisdom." Wisdom, therefore, is the fear of the Lord. God says what He means, and means what He says; and when it is repeated, it is worthy of notation.

CHAPTER TWO

Three Main Types Of Godly Wisdom

All of us have the wisdom of God in our spirit. When you receive Christ into your heart, you also receive the wisdom of God, which is hidden in Christ.

There are three main types of Godly wisdom revealed in these Greek words thus:

"Sophia" - Wisdom

"Sunesis" - Understanding, Knowledge

"Phronesis" - Practical wisdom

Sophia, according to Wikipedia, is the "ability to think and act using knowledge, experience, understanding, common sense and insight." It is also a central idea. It is a theoretical wisdom, which comes with the gospel. 1st Corinthians 1:30 says, "But of Him are ye in Christ Jesus, who of God is made unto us wisdom, and righteousness, and sanctification, and redemption." An example of this wisdom is revealed in this scenario: You recently moved into a new neighborhood with your family. A friend told you there is a good school for your kids about 15 minutes away from your home. You got excited and agreed to check it out. Meanwhile, there is another school, just 5 minutes away from your place, but its reputation is not as good as the other one. You never made out time to explore the possibility of getting them into it until it was too late. So, it remained a good mental idea to get them into that better school, but you never followed up the process, to make it a reality.

Sunesis, is the Greek word for "Understanding or Knowledge." This knowledge is analytical or critical wisdom, which is mentally explored. Here, you give an in-depth consideration on any issue before taking an action. Luke 2:47 says, "And all that heard Him were astonished at His understanding and answers." With Sunesis, you may know what to do in a particular situation and still not do it. You may know the various quicker routes to get to your church and still not go. Why? You continue vacillating between going through the inner city roads or the beltway; waiting for another 15mins to catch a power nap before heading out to your car; thinking whether to stop at the gas station to fill your gas tank and now looking at your time, realizing it will be too late before you get to church decided not to go anymore. You kept analyzing it and never made an effort. You refused to apply energy or force to make you get up and do the needful.

Phronesis, is the Greek word for "wisdom" or intelligence, according to Wikipedia. "It is more specifically, a type of wisdom relevant to practical things, requiring an ability to discern how or why to act virtuously and encourage practical virtue, excellence of character in others." This high level of wisdom was evidenced in the life of King Solomon, known to be the wisest man that ever lived. 1Kings 10: 23-24 says, "So King Solomon exceeded all the kings of the earth for riches and for wisdom. And all the earth sought to Solomon, to hear his wisdom, which God had put in his heart." This God - endowment gave him a "distinguishing mark" in his life time. Not only did he have an elevated mind, he put in effort, energy to develop himself, so he could maximize his God-given wisdom, manage his national affairs properly and be a blessing to his generation. The Scripture says in 1Kings 4:29, "And God gave Solomon wisdom and understanding exceeding much, and largeness of heart, even as the sand that is on the sea shore." His elevated thinking made his reasoning, vocabulary, communication and execution of projects to be profound. Phronesis, ultimately, not only gives you the ability to obtain knowledge, but empowers you through the use of effort and energy, to apply the knowledge you have acquired. While some ideas (Sophia) may have been stimulated in your mind during the process of knowledge acquisition, it is important to consciously dig deeper using analytical wisdom (Sunesis) to know how best to dive into the idea. However, do not stop there, but go all the way to practical wisdom (Phronesis), which is the actual doing of something, rather than leaving it in the realm of theory, ideas and analysis. This book project is a good example of the application of the three levels of wisdom. At the beginning, I had it as an idea; then I progressed to analyzing what the entire process would require; I then put in effort and energy even when I didn't feel like writing, to bring it to completion. Practical wisdom propels you to *do something*. Today, vision is reality, because of the Power of Practical wisdom - Phronesis.

CHAPTER THREE

Where Can Wisdom Be Found?

It may seem that wisdom can't be found. No man knows where wisdom can be found. Even the writer in Job 28:12-14 asks, "But where shall wisdom be found, and where is the place of understanding?" The depth saith, "It is not in me: and the sea saith, It is not with me." He continued with his question in Job 28:20-22 by asking again, "From where then does wisdom come, and where is the place of understanding? It is hidden from the eyes of all living, and the knowledge of it is withheld from the birds of the heavens, Abaddon (the place of destruction), and death says, we have only heard the report of it with our ears." However, the next verse is a great revelation on where Wisdom can be found! Job 28:23 says, "God understands the way (to Wisdom), and He knows the place of it, *(Wisdom is with God alone!)*. This means there is a way to get to Wisdom, not any kind of way (only God's way), and there is a place for it too. Wisdom sure has a residence, and it is with God alone!

Why Is Wisdom Found In God Alone?

Our asking why wisdom is found alone in God is like asking, "Why is the fish found only in water?" As water is the natural habitat for the fish, so is God the residence of wisdom. No fish can survive outside water, as they will suffocate due to inability to breathe. The body of the fish needs to have water to get oxygen to survive with the help of its gills; the human body needs air in order to breathe, with the help of its lungs; so does wisdom need a God environment to thrive. Wisdom, *manifests* in its fullness, *only in God!*

Job 12:13 says, "With Him is wisdom and strength, He hath counsel and understanding." In the Daniel 2:20, he said, "Blessed be the name of God forever and ever, for wisdom and might are His." Not only is God the source of wisdom, He is Himself, Wisdom! God's wisdom is far superior to our human wisdom. A life outside the wisdom of God will be in total disarray!

Why Is Wisdom the Principal Thing?

Wisdom is the principal thing, the essence, the important thing, the pre-eminent thing, the foremost thing. It is the principal thing because it is the authentic Word of God. It is the principal thing because it is the precise Word of God. Wisdom is our navigation system in life. Wisdom is a defense, wisdom is a deliverer, wisdom is your epiphany, wisdom is everything! It delivers you from taking detours in life. The writer in Proverbs 1:21 continuously declares that wisdom stands at intersections, roof tops, and very strategic places; to warn people ahead of time on what to do, what not to do; what to say, what not to say; where to go, and where not to go. If we genuinely look back into our lives, there are many things we did because we lacked wisdom at the time. However, it is refreshing to know according to James 1:5, that God is not only willing, but able to give wisdom to anyone that lacks it. God is all seeing and all knowing. None of us is a surprise to God. If we begin today to walk in His wisdom, He will condense time for us. He has a way of doing things that will shock you, and those around you. 1st Corinthians 2:9 states, "But as it is written, Eye hath not seen, nor ear heard, neither have entered into the heart of man, the things which God hath prepared for them that love Him." There is a thing that has been prepared for those that love God. All we need is to have the courage to obey Him. It sure does take courage to obey God. There is a preparation, there is a plan, and there is a process, to our becoming the ultimate God-product. He is able to move you from the back to the front, with a blast of his nostrils, or by just sneezing. The good news about wisdom is that it teaches you *it is never too late to do the right thing!* None of us can go back, and make a new beginning, but each of us can *start* from where we are, and *make* a happy ending!

CHAPTER FOUR

When Should Wisdom Be Applied?

Godly and skillful wisdom will let you know when to speak, or be quiet. I'm learning daily that it's not enough to have wisdom, the application is very critical. If you use what I call "wisdom of the morning" and apply it at noon time, or night time; it will neither be effective, nor fruitful. While wisdom is very key, it is important to skillfully introduce it at the right time, to elicit the desired response. Timing of wisdom application should never be glossed over. It is the wisdom of God that made Peter, the apostle, on the day of Pentecost speak up, and boldly declared they were not drunk in the midst of jeering and mocking by the devout Jews that had gathered. He spoke up at the right time. Peter confidently continued; explaining that what they were witnessing was rather the fulfillment of what the Prophet Joel had declared earlier to them. He had said in the last days, "God will pour out His Spirit on all flesh, and your sons and daughters shall prophesy." (Acts 2:14-36; Joel 2:28-32). This led to 3000 men giving their lives to Christ, in one day! Remember, none of the other apostles spoke up, only Peter. What an amazing response, all because of Godly and skillful wisdom! This truly made me pause to think, and reflect on how truly our words, inspired by God, can create feelings for others, making them tender, even in the face of intense hurt, bitterness and opposition. It's usually not what we say that counts; it is the "how" that makes all the difference. Perhaps, that's why Ecclesiastes 1:1 says, "For everything there is a season." For instance, in giving wise counsel, give it only if asked, otherwise you will be doing it out of season. Not only will it not be received well nor appreciated, but you will also be wasting your words, and your precious time. Growing up, my father used to say to us children, "In life, anyone can do whatever they choose to do, but the only thing they are never free to choose are the consequences of their actions." While it's good to give counsel to friends, family and those you love, especially when you sense a huge challenge on a decision they are about to make, be wise in your timing. If the timing is not right, learn to leave it alone. It may be a God- ordained learning curve, good or bad, for all parties involved. Wisdom teaches an undeniable truth that, not only is timing golden, it is everything!

CHAPTER FIVE

Who Qualifies To Seek For Wisdom?

Wisdom is for the hungry; only the hungry can be fed. You can't feed someone that is not hungry. Wisdom is not for those who think they know it all. It's not for those who think it's only their opinion that counts in everything. Why is it so? It is so because Proverbs15:22 says, "Plans fail for lack of counsel, but with many advisers they succeed." I once heard that, "*Even the dumb and the ignorant, they too have their story.*" Matthew 5:6 says, "Blessed are they which do hunger, and thirst after righteousness: for they shall be filled." Wisdom teaches you to be righteousness conscious. Those who are willing to plant the seed of wisdom, which is humility, will be bestowed with wisdom. This is because humility will bring you to the point where you will understand that, you don't know everything. It is still okay not to know everything. No matter how much you think you know, there are people who still know more than you. *You never know what you don't know, until you listen!* It takes courage to listen, but it is still good to do so. It's like allowing yourself to be deceived by thinking that you are the most beautiful thing that hit the earth. Don't forget, the beautiful ones are not yet born! Recognizing, and agreeing that there are things you don't know, is a mark of strength. It's only the weak and the insecure, who are not able to seek out wise counsel in the midst of obvious confusion and danger. Ecclesiastes 7:19 says, "True wisdom is strength to the wise, more than ten rulers or valiant generals who are in the city." Learning is continuous, and the day we quit learning, we die. It is only wisdom that will make you know it's time to come down from your high horse, and genuinely seek wisdom to identify whatever challenges you may be facing; confront it, and then conquer it. What you don't identify as an issue, will never be confronted, and what you never confront, will never be conquered. Wisdom will walk you through the inherent pain in the process of seeking, and reaching for the truth. John 8:32 declares, "And you shall know the truth and the truth shall make you free." Truth has only one destination, and it is called, "The Land of Freedom!"

Why Pursue Wisdom?

Wisdom is the game changer! Wisdom brings you to the table of truth. As games cannot be won unless they are played, so wisdom cannot be found unless it is sought after. Proverbs 19:21 says, "Many plans are in a man's mind, but it is the Lord's purpose for him that will stand." Wisdom reveals purpose, God's original intent for each of our lives. Is any other thing more worthy of our pursuit than Godly and skillful wisdom? Wisdom not only gives us strength, it is our bridge over every troubled water in our lives. Wisdom is our peace. Wisdom keeps us always in the eye of the storm. Where there is wisdom, there is honor. Proverbs 4:9 says, "Wisdom will give to your neck a wreath of gracefulness, a crown of beauty and glory will she deliver to you." Wisdom teaches you to *compete with yourself* and not with others. Have a plan for improvement. Be intentional about your growth. Determine not to be where you are today, tomorrow. While it is good sometimes to compare yourself with another person's seeming success, be sure your motive is pure. Ask the successful person questions that could help you with areas you are struggling with. Be honest with yourself. We are to *complement* one another, not be in *competition* with them. Competing with others lead to frustration, envy, jealousy and acrimony. It is a huge distraction! Wisdom asks, "Why envy another?" An old adage says, "*Envy no man, for you know not his or her secret grieves!*" The grass looks greener on the other side of the fence, until you show up there. Remember, you are not called to be like others, or do what they do. You are called to be you; so make a conscious effort to be the original and authentic you. Psalm 139:14 says, "You are fearfully and wonderfully made." Learn from others, but don't be like them or become them. You lose your God-given unique flavor when you do so. Wisdom helps you to always correct your focus, and be consistent in your commitment. Consistency, or constancy of purpose, is and remains the secret of real success, and it is only revealed by wisdom. Learn to run your own race with grace and confidence! Learn to do well in your own race!

CHAPTER SIX

How Can We Get Wisdom?

Children resemble their parents. They have the DNA of their parents. We reproduce who we are, and we reproduce what we are. We cannot give what we don't have. We become what we behold. We become what we believe. We are made in the image and likeness of God. In His image, we look like Him; in His likeness, we function like Him. One of His functions is that He is a creative God; since we are made in His likeness, we have creative abilities too. God is limitless Wisdom; looking up to Him, is key to getting Wisdom. The God of Wisdom never changes; He was yesterday, He is still today, and forever will be. It is sad that most of us are not walking in the reality of who we are. We don't even know we have a Father, who is Wisdom personified. We are looking for wisdom in all the nooks and corners, and leaving out the first place we should inquire of wisdom. No wonder we are maimed in the battlefield of life and get ourselves into a huge quagmire because of lack of wisdom.

In life, we keep telling people what they need to do or how to get what is required of them, but the issue is, they may not know what to do or how to get what is expected from them. I'm quite sure some reading this book may be wondering, so what do I need to do to get this wisdom? How do I go about it? Matthew 7:7 says, "Ask, it shall be given to you, seek, and you shall find; knock, and the door will be opened to you." God cannot lie. His resume is unchanging. He is eternally the same. Do you know, how you go about getting any other thing you desire, is how you also go about getting wisdom. Say you desperately need a green suit for an event, and you've searched in all the stores close to you without success, now you are confused, as to where next to go looking for it. A friend shows up that evening, and you share your despair. She informs you there's a store twenty miles away. They have the exact suit you want, and there's only one left. What will you do? I'm sure you will find out how early the store opens. You want to be there just before they open. You don't mind waiting outside. You don't want anyone beating you to the purchase of this suit. You do whatever it takes to get it, and you are happy. Getting wisdom is the same. You have to first of all, make up your mind that you want wisdom. How bad do you want it? How desperate are you? God is Wisdom. Proverbs 2:6 declares, "The Lord gives skillful and Godly wisdom; from His mouth come knowledge and understanding." Revelation 3:20 says, "Behold, I stand at the door, and knock: if any man hears my voice, and open the door, I will come in to him, and will sup with him, and he with me." If God says He will come in, He *will* come in. Receive courage to invite Him in, open up your bible, read it, study it, and remember, He inspired men of old to write the bible. God is a writer, God is a Teacher, and He is the giver of all wisdom. May the scepter of His wisdom be stretched out to you today! You can pray in your own words, or use this simple prayer below as a guide:

Lord, I'm here for you today;
I acknowledge I lack your wisdom;
my case is based on your Word. God,
you said in Proverbs 1:23, if I repent,
you will pour out your Spirit of Wisdom
upon me, and make known your words to me.
Lord, I ask,
let your mercy be abundant on me;

make me today a receiver of your limitless wisdom, in Jesus Mighty Name,

Amen!

CHAPTER SEVEN

What Is In It For Me?

Anything we do in life, we want to know what is in it for us. Some of us will be asking, what is in it for me? Why seek after wisdom? You know, it makes good sense for each of us to go to work daily. Why? We want to get paid, and to take care of our needs. Great! It will also make sense for us to go to school, to be certified in any field we want to work in as a career, so that we are able to put food on the table, and go even further. Guess what! Wisdom is the driver!! You stand to gain a lot in your lifetime when you reach out to wisdom. Isaiah 14:24 says, "The Lord of hosts hath sworn, saying, surely as I have thought, so shall it come to pass; and as I have purposed, so shall it stand." If God says, Wisdom is the principal thing, it is what He says it is. If He says it is the principal thing, then what is in it for you, is the principal thing! Wisdom is your essence. It reveals the original and authentic you. Passionate seeking of wisdom leaves its residue on you. In life, you become what you behold or what you look at. You are what you eat. Eat wisdom, and you will flow in wisdom. In-depth searching for wisdom will guide you to consciously review, whether you are actually becoming what you are beholding. Most of us have great role models, however, you need to take time and assess, whether you are doing what it takes, to become who you want to be or you are leaving it to chance. It is wisdom that empowers you to develop the discipline required to become what you believe. It is also not enough to want to become what you are looking at; another critical issue is, when you become that you have been dreaming about, what is your sustenance or maintenance capability? Can you maintain what you are becoming? Most people become, but lose it overnight due to inability to maintain what or who they have become. Character garnered from wisdom is the keeping power. That is one of the benefits of wisdom. You can have the fame or notoriety of your role model that has spanned over many decades, for only six months, due to inability to maintain what you may have become. Wisdom will also make you know that when you have realized your dream, it is important to share it with others. You can also share it in bits as it is revealed to you. Habakkuk 2:2 says, "And the Lord answered me and said, write the vision and make it plain upon tables, that he may run that readeth it." *You cannot read what is not written, and you cannot run with what is not read and understood.* Sharing your vision can inspire others to do greater things with their lives. Doing so will make you become a distribution channel of hope, touching and changing lives. Wisdom also prompts you to occasionally slow down yourself, so you can speed up yourself. Always endeavor to immerse yourself beyond yourself in the Wisdom of God, as it will take you to places you will never be able to get to on your own. Wisdom will always guide you in making right choices. Even if you have been living a mistake in the past; wisdom will take you by the hand, and get you to where God had always prepared for you. Where there is no wisdom, detours are inevitable. Wisdom is our navigation system. It helps us enjoy our journey through life, and ultimately become fulfilled every step of the way. When you latch on to wisdom, *your best days are ahead of you, not behind you!*

Why He Left His Book –The Bible

Imagine you bought a television set from the store, got home and excitedly started setting it up, got stuck and reached for the manufacturer's manual in the box, only to realize it was not included in the packaging! You are now frustrated because you cannot figure out the next step in the set up without the manual. What do you do? The only way out is to get in touch with the store, to see if they have any manual handy, or you call the manufacturer to rush one to you. Either way, you desperately need the manufacturer's manual to complete your set up. So, can you see, this is why God left His Book? When we get stuck in our life's journey, we have a fall back, a God Resource manual. In any situation, He comes through for us. We call on Him, not only because He has the manual, He is the Manual! Connect with Him through reading and studying His Word, and He will be your anchor on this life's ocean. We can't navigate life safely without Him. Trying to do so will be futile every step of the way. God is limitless Wisdom! God made us in His image and in His likeness. He *gave* us His Word, to *make* us His Word. We are *Word Practitioners* on this earth! Never forget He is The Word. Let's be wise and mine the *treasures* He left for us, in His Book!

CONCLUSION

Wisdom Corner

Three Pre-requisites for Wisdom

The *HOW* acronym qualifies you to be multiplied in the Wisdom of God:

H - ***Humility*** - is genuinely and unashamedly, acknowledging you don't know, and need God's guidance.

O - ***Obsession*** - The proof of desire is pursuit. You pursue what you desire. When you either want His guidance, or nothing else, it shows you are desperate for His Wisdom.

W - ***Waiting*** - God cannot be rushed. Wait with patience; wait with expectation. Wait on Him in His Word. Study and meditate on His Word intensely. Joshua 1:8

says, "This book of the law shall not depart out of thy mouth; but thou shalt meditate on it day and night; that thou may observe to do according to all that is written therein; for then thou shalt make thy way prosperous, and then thou shalt have good success."

12 Nuggets of Wisdom

- Wisdom brings you to the table of truth.
- Wisdom teaches you to embrace forgiveness and move forward.
- Wisdom is your life's navigation system.
- Wisdom keeps you rooted in humility.
- Wisdom crowns you with grace, prestige and honor.
- Wisdom reveals it's never too late, to do the right thing.
- Wisdom teaches that none of us can go back and make a new beginning; but each of us can start from where we are, and make a happy ending.
- Wisdom reveals that everyone you meet is a door; be wise with your relationships. Great opportunities may be lurking behind them.
- Where there is wisdom, there is root, and where there is root, there is fruit. So, be wise.
- Wisdom alerts us we are not called to be busy; we are called to be fruitful.
- Wisdom teaches there is a difference between deciding and doing.

- In wisdom, purpose is unveiled, because where purpose is not known, abuse is inevitable.

Wisdom – The Voice of Value

Three girls are standing at the edge of an indoor pool. Two decide to jump into the pool. How many are left? Some may say one, but the correct answer is *three*. Never forget that there is a great difference between deciding and doing! So, what's your stand on all your dreams and visions? Do you still want to leave them in the realm of ideas and critical wisdom? Why not start today to apply practical wisdom in all you do? Doing so will set you up, to evolve into who you could never have imagined. I encourage you today, *to get a good and deep sense, of who you are. Let the dreams come alive again! Tell your heart, to beat again!* Remember, it's never too late to become, what you believe! You are your only limitation.

DAILY AFFIRMATIONS

THE EXTRAORDINARY WOMAN

I am an Extraordinary WOMAN in Christ Jesus

I have Great Power

I will do Great Things in God

I see the Invisible

I believe the Impossible

I will do the Incredible

I have the Heart of a Champion

The mind of a Winner

And

I possess, the Spirit of a Conqueror!

* * *

THE EXTRAORDINARY MAN

I am an Extraordinary MAN in Christ Jesus

I have Great Power

I will do Great Things in God

I see the Invisible

I believe the Impossible

I will do the Incredible

I have the Heart of a Champion

The mind of a Winner

And

I possess, the Spirit of a Conqueror!

* * *

Acknowledgement

Life has taught me that no one can be led by their instincts without encouragement, support and influence from their family, friends and many more. I'm a strong advocate of the statement that, "No one man has ever done anything great, all by himself." In life, you need a team, whether formal or informal!

I'm delighted to say that this book is a product of love in action. I gratefully acknowledge each and everyone for their enormous sacrifice, contributions, to this book. Your friendship is a joy to me.

I feel a deep sense of gratitude to:

-*Jamel Kornegay,* your ability to capture the essence of my heart in the book cover design is a unique work of providence. Your continuous support helps make it easy for me to fulfill God's will.

-*Bisi Oladipo,* your make-up artistic skill evidenced in the book cover picture, made this book look better.

-*Miriam Mendez and Jahshua Blyden,* your efforts to make this book better through your editorial expertise and insight brought this work to life.

-*Eli Blyden* and the entire CrunchTime Graphics team, my deep appreciation to you, for formatting, embracing and supporting my work with great respect.

-My gratitude to *Maryellen O'Rourke and A&A Printing,* my publishing family, for the printing, publishing and production of this book.

About The Author

Henrietta C. Ekekezie
Author, Speaker, Empowerment Coach

Born in Nigeria, West Africa, Henrietta, is the President and Founder of Refreshing Glory Ministries Inc., a People Empowerment Ministry that is dedicated to developing, and empowering women from all nations, to reach their highest potential, through the vehicle of prayer. Her philosophy that, "where you are, is not who you are" encourages women to maximize their capabilities and attain quality growth spiritually, mentally, emotionally and physically. She is committed to helping invest women with power to become what they believe.

She is also a Prayer Intercessor, Teacher and Retreat/Conference Organizer.

Major facets of her ministry are: Power Prayer sessions, Bible Study Fellowships, Retreats and Empowerment Seminars and Outreaches where she offers quality teachings for effective spiritual growth. Her meetings are characterized with an atmosphere filled with the Refreshing Glory and Presence of God, inspiring people they are meant for more, and to actively discover their unique God-given purpose through seeking the wisdom of God in prayer. An additional component to her portfolio includes teaching and developing women to consciously cultivate and lead change that is Godly, through intentional growth. Through Refreshing Glory Ministries, she is extensively involved with other ministries where she serves on several committees. She is also the Vision Leader of SPIRITUAL KITCHEN, a vision that embraces women from all nations and works of life, coming together to intercede in prayer for all, and empower both young and old.

Some of her educational background include; Bachelor of Education degree with a major in English Language, Bachelor of Science degree in Nursing, and a Master of Science degree in Organizational Leadership.

How To Contact The Author

~

To reach Henrietta C. Ekekezie,
founder of Refreshing Glory Ministries,
regarding a speaking engagement,
upcoming events: seminars, conferences, retreats and
empowerment outreaches,
or to read about her upcoming books and
other ministry products,

please visit her website at:
Web: ***www.refreshinggloryministries.org***
Email: ***info@refreshinggloryministries.org***
Phone: ***1-888-247-0478***

Or write to mailing address:
10482 Baltimore Avenue Suite 114
Beltsville, MD 20705

~